Mountains

by Sheila Anderson

first step nonfiction

Lerner Publications Company · Minneapolis

What is a **mountain?**

It is a kind of **landform.**

A mountain is land that rises toward the sky.

Mountains are taller than
the land around them.

There are mountains in the
ocean. These are **islands.**

Many **volcanoes** are mountains.

Some mountains have
pointed tops.

Some mountains have
rounded tops.

Some mountains are rocky.

Many mountains have snow on top.

Animals live on mountains.

Plants grow on mountains.

People live on mountains.

People **climb** mountains.

There are many things to do on a mountain.

Would you like to explore
a mountain?

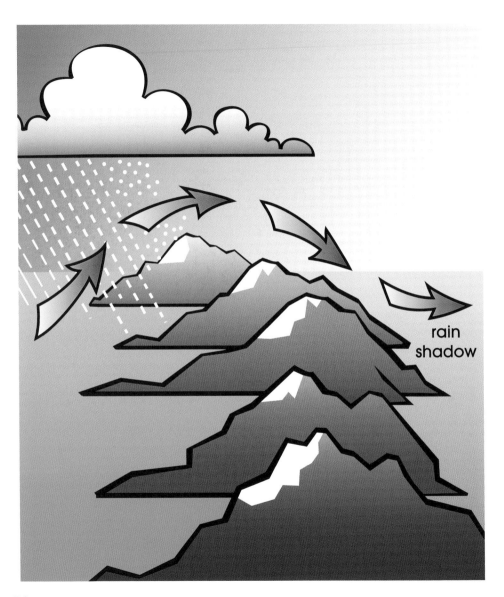

rain shadow

Rain Shadow

Do you know what a rain shadow is? It is the area on one side of a mountain that gets very little rain.

Mountains help make rain shadows. When clouds blow over mountains, they cool. The water in the clouds falls as rain or snow.

By the time the cloud is over the mountain, most of the water is gone. So the other side of the mountain gets very little rain. It becomes a rain shadow.

Mountain Facts

 The outer part of the earth is called the crust. Some mountains are formed when two pieces of the earth's crust push against each other. They push the land up, making a mountain.

 Some mountains are formed when hot lava from deep within the earth comes out a crack in the earth's crust. It flows up and out, and then cools, forming a mound.

The world's highest mountain is Mount Everest. It is in Asia.

 The highest mountain in North America is Mount McKinley. It is in the state of Alaska, which is part of the United States.

 The air high up in the sky is cooler than the air close to the earth, so some mountain tops are cold and have snow all year round.

Glossary

 climb – to go up, down, or over using hands and feet

 islands – pieces of land that have water on all sides

 landform – a natural feature of the earth's surface

 mountain – a piece of land that is taller than a hill

 volcanoes – breaks in the earth's surface where hot, melted rock called lava flows out

Index

The photographs in this book are reproduced with the permission of: © Mary Liz Austin/Image Bank/Getty Images, pp. 2, 22 (second from bottom); © Prisma/SuperStock, pp. 3, 22 (middle); © Peter Van Rhijn/SuperStock, p. 4; © Rod Barbee/Visuals Unlimited, p. 5; © Dick Roberts/Visuals Unlimited, pp. 6, 22 (second from top); © age fotostock/SuperStock, pp. 7, 11, 17, 22 (bottom); © Gary Brettnacher/SuperStock, p. 8; PhotoDisc Royalty-Free by Getty Images, pp. 9, 12; © Steve Vidler/SuperStock, p. 10; © Willard Clay/Photographer's Choice/Getty Images, p. 13; © Dennis Flaherty/Photographer's Choice/Getty Images, p. 14; © Pierre Jacques/Getty Images, pp. 15, 22 (top); © Photononstop/SuperStock, p. 16.

Front Cover: © Richard Price/Taxi/Getty Images.

Illustration on page 18 by Laura Westlund/Independent Picture Service.

Lerner Publications Company
A division of Lerner Publishing Group, Inc.
241 First Avenue North
Minneapolis, MN 55401 U.S.A.

Website address: www.lernerbooks.com

Library of Congress Cataloging-in-Publication Data

Anderson, Sheila.
    Mountains / by Sheila Anderson.
        p.   cm. — (First step nonfiction. Landforms)
    Includes index.
    ISBN: 978–0–8225–8590–9 (lib. bdg. : alk. paper)
    1. Mountains—Juvenile literature. 2. Mountain ecology—Juvenile literature. I. Title.
GB512.A53 2008
551.43′2—dc22   2007007814

Manufactured in the United States of America
1 2 3 4 5 6 – DP – 13 12 11 10 09 08